Do You KNOW?

THE AMERICAN REVOLUTION

A revolutionary quiz about the rebels,
rabble-rousers, battles and founders

Guy Robinson

D1415028

SOURCEBOOKS, INC.®
NAPERVILLE, ILLINOIS

Copyright © 2007 by Carlinsky & Carlinsky, Inc.
Cover and internal design © 2007 by Sourcebooks, Inc.

Published by Sourcebooks, Inc.
P.O. Box 4410, Naperville, Illinois 60567-4410
(630) 961-3900
Fax: (630) 961-2168
www.sourcebooks.com

ISBN-13: 978-1-4022-1233-8
ISBN-10: 1-4022-1233-X

Printed and bound in the United States of America
SP 10 9 8 7 6 5 4 3 2 1

This is *not* your history teacher's quiz book! It's a fast-moving, broad-ranging test on the full Revolutionary period in America: the scene-setting time as Britain tightens the reins, the boiling over, the military encounters up and down the colonies, and the Constitution-building years as the new nation gets ready to rev its engines and hit the road. But the mix and flavor of questions makes this test more colorful—and more challenging—than the typical Friday-morning pop quiz.

There's no attempt to exhaust any topic, or to cover every base in this rich, complicated time in the country's history. Instead, you'll face quick questions that hop from meeting rooms to battlefields, from names to numbers, dealing with songs and poems, generals and geniuses, patriots and traitors of the Revolution. With a range like that, it won't be easy. By the time you finish, not only will you have seen how much you know and don't know, but you may find that you've discovered an aspect or two that you'd like to go off and explore to learn more.

So here are 100 questions. Count ten points for each correct answer. Where a question has more than one part, you'll be told how to divide the credit. Here and there you'll find a chance to earn five or ten bonus points, so it's theoretically possible to score more than 1,000. (But you won't!)

Figure your performance this way:

Above 900:	**Spectacular!**
700–899:	A very solid showing
500–699:	Nothing to be ashamed of
Below 500:	Told you it was tough

1. In the 17th and 18th centuries, the British Parliament passed a series of acts regulating and restricting trade and manufacturing in the American colonies. Which *wasn't* one of those acts?

   a. The Hat Act
   b. The Woolen Act
   c. The Lace and Linen Act
   d. The Iron Act
   e. The Sugar Act

2. What 1765 law affected not only manufacturers and traders, but all citizens in the colonies, because it taxed such things as newspapers, playing cards, and legal documents?

   _____

3. The secret organizations that sprung up to resist British authority, sometimes with violent protests, were known as the _____ _____ _____. (For ten bonus points, say where the name came from.)

4. The Townshend Acts of 1767, which taxed tea and other imports, were named for:

   a. Robert Townshend, the Governor General of Massachusetts Bay Colony
   b. Charles Townshend, the British Chancellor of the Exchequer
   c. Big Tree Townshend, a Narragansett chief who supported the Crown and took an English surname
   d. Peter Townshend, a politically connected British tea trader and composer

5. In 1768, a ship owned by a Boston trader who was in the habit of smuggling goods from England to avoid import taxes was nabbed by British customs, leading to rioting among disappointed customers and Patriots. Who was the smuggler?

   a. Samuel Adams
   b. John Adams
   c. Crispus Attucks
   d. John Hancock

6. How many deaths resulted from The Boston Massacre, in which British troops fired on a growing mob of hostile civilians?

    a. 5
    b. 55
    c. 96
    d. 296

7. Following the Boston riot, England:

    a. increased the number of troops assigned to the city
    b. ordered troops in Boston not to carry muskets except in case of battle
    c. moved troops from downtown to an island in Boston Harbor
    d. made no changes at all

8. What name was given to the inter-colony communication organizations started in 1772 that helped pave the way for the First Continental Congress?

_____

9. After Parliament passed the Tea Act in 1773, giving favorable treatment to the powerful East India Company, the company began to send boatloads of tea to America. Ten points for the name of any of the first three ships that arrived at Boston Harbor; ten bonus points if you can name another one; ten more if you know them all.

_____

10. On December 16, 1773, a band of patriots boarded three newly arrived ships and dumped their cargos of tea into Boston Harbor. The protestors were dressed and made up to look like:

    a. British lords
    b. Pirates
    c. American Indians
    d. Ghosts

11. **Boston had its Tea Party. In New York and Philadelphia, activists saw to it that dockworkers forced the East India Company ships to sail back to England without unloading their cargo. What happened in Charleston?**

    a. The tea was sent back, just as happened in New York and Philadelphia
    b. The tea was dumped, just as happened in Boston
    c. The tea was locked in warehouses at the dock
    d. The tea was delivered without problems

12. **What *didn't* the British authorities order in June 1774, in retaliation for the Boston Tea Party and other acts of unrest?**

    a. Taxes on tea and other supplies doubled
    b. Boston's port to be closed until the tea was paid for
    c. Massachusetts legislature to be weakened and colony-wide officials to be chosen by the King or the British governor
    d. British troops to be quartered in private homes anywhere in the 13 colonies

13. **The British called the laws meant to tighten control on restless colonists the Coercive Acts. What did the colonists call them?**

_____

14. **Unhappy colonists arranged a conference of delegates from all the colonies, the First Continental Congress, held in September and October 1774. In what city did this series of meetings take place?**

_____

15. **The First Continental Congress attracted 55 delegates from 12 of the 13 colonies. Which colony failed to send a delegate?**

    a. Vermont
    b. Georgia
    c. Rhode Island
    d. New Jersey

16. At its conclusion, the First Continental Congress issued a document called the Articles of Association, containing a list of grievances and an agreement to stand together to boycott British imports. Who was the paper's first signer—in the "John Hancock" position?

_____

17. On an April night in 1775, two lanterns were lit in Boston's Old North Church, signifying that the British regulars were riding "by sea." How long were the lights left burning?

   a. a few minutes
   b. an hour
   c. all night
   d. until after the Battle of Concord the next day

18. Notwithstanding two centuries of good press, starting with the Longfellow poem, Paul Revere did not ride alone. Who also went to Lexington, by another route, and met him there? (Ten-point bonus: Name the third rider, a physician they met after they left Lexington, on the way to Concord.) _____

_____

19. What did Thomas Gage, Britain's North American commander-in-chief, think his wife might have done, and what did he do about it?

_____

_____

20. Who first used the expression "the shot heard 'round the world," referring to the opening of the Battle of Concord?

   a. Paul Revere
   b. An unknown Patriot soldier
   c. An unknown British regular
   d. A poet

21. At the time of the Revolution, the population of the American colonies was about:

    a. 1 million
    b. 2.5 million
    c. 5 million
    d. 7.5 million

22. The Battle of Bunker Hill was fought mainly around a nearby fort, where the Americans ran out of ammunition and were forced to flee to Bunker Hill. Where was most of the action?

_____

23. What famous order did an officer who was acutely aware of the ammunition shortage supposedly give during that battle?

_____

24. After the Battle of Bunker Hill, General Gage was called home to England. What happened when he got there?

    a. He was blamed for letting the rebellion get out of hand and relieved of his post
    b. He was told to shape up or ship out
    c. He was told to take a month's rest and get back to fighting
    d. He found no one in the government to talk to and sailed back to America

25. One of the early Patriot victories was at Fort Ticonderoga, New York, taken by Ethan Allen and Benedict Arnold and a small pack who called themselves the Green Mountain Boys of Vermont. How many died during the takeover?

_____

26. When the American Revolution broke out, George III had been king:

    a. Only a month
    b. Since 1770
    c. Since 1760
    d. Since 1750

27. Throughout the Revolution, the King never issued a formal statement that mentioned the rebels. True or false?

    _____

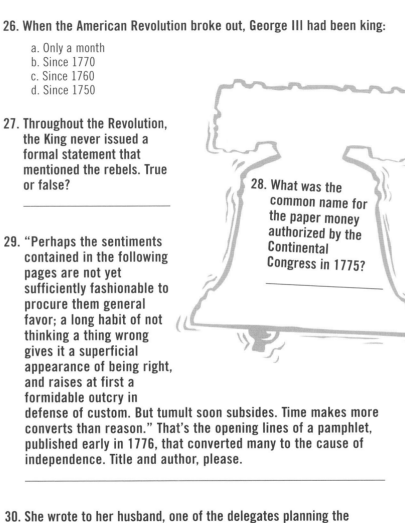

28. What was the common name for the paper money authorized by the Continental Congress in 1775?

    _____

29. "Perhaps the sentiments contained in the following pages are not yet sufficiently fashionable to procure them general favor; a long habit of not thinking a thing wrong gives it a superficial appearance of being right, and raises at first a formidable outcry in defense of custom. But tumult soon subsides. Time makes more converts than reason." That's the opening lines of a pamphlet, published early in 1776, that converted many to the cause of independence. Title and author, please.

    _____

30. She wrote to her husband, one of the delegates planning the workings of the new nation, beseeching him to "remember the ladies, and be more generous and favorable to them than your ancestors." Who was she? _____

31. A Committee of Five, chosen to draft the Declaration of Independence, gave the job to Thomas Jefferson. Who *wasn't* on that drafting committee?

   a. John Adams
   b. Benjamin Franklin
   c. Robert Livingston
   d. James Madison
   e. Roger Sherman

32. What state document was Jefferson's model and inspiration when he composed the Declaration? (For ten bonus points: Who wrote it?) _____

33. Which one of these bits of quotes is *not* in the Declaration of Independence?

   a. "all men are created equal"
   b. "life, liberty, and the pursuit of happiness"
   c. "deriving their just powers from the consent of the governed"
   d. "promote the general welfare and secure the blessings of liberty to ourselves and our posterity"
   e. "United States of America"

34. Fifty-six men signed the Declaration. For two points apiece, who are these five signers?

   a. He became president _____
   b. He became president, too _____
   c. He signed and then spent most of the next nine years in Paris

   _____
   d. An insurance company is named for him _____
   e. A beer is named for him _____

35. One Rhode Island delegate signed with a physical condition that made his hand shake. "My hand trembles," he remarked, "but my heart does not." His name? _____

36. The Liberty Bell in Philadelphia, which probably wasn't rung to announce a reading of the Declaration, actually was rung on some other important occasions, such as the opening of the First Continental Congress. The bell now carries an inscription: "PROCLAIM LIBERTY THROUGHOUT ALL THE LAND UNTO THE INHABITANTS THEREOF." What's the source of that quote?

_____

37. Who was sent by the Continental Congress to Paris in 1776 to arrange secret arms deals? _____

38. How was the French supplier to be paid?

    a. Gold ingots
    b. Shillings
    c. Continental notes to come due after the war
    d. Tobacco

39. Before they retreated across the Delaware River after losing New York to the British late in 1776, what did Washington and his forces do to try to hold off the advancing Redcoats?

_____

40. Knowing that as Washington retreated across New Jersey the British would eventually get to Philadelphia (where they were meeting), to what city did the Continental Congress move?

    a. Richmond
    b. Baltimore
    c. Annapolis
    d. Harrisburg

41. Name the double agent who, pretending to be a Tory sympathizer, fed information to Washington and brought misleading reports back to the British, setting the stage for the Christmas Eve Battle of Trenton, the first big American victory of the war.

_____

42. Which two of these upgrades ordered late in 1776 bolstered the Continental Army's performance in the following years?

   a. Enlistments to be for three years or "for the war," rather than for one year
   b. Troops to come from each colony according to population, rather than heavily from the New England area
   c. Officers to receive special month-long training course before assuming command
   d. Local women required to prepare and deliver nutritious meals to troops in the field

43. How old was Lafayette when Congress made him a general in the Continental Army? _____

44. The Marquis de Lafayette, as he was known, wasn't really a marquis—that was an honorific bestowed upon him by his troops in the colonies. In fact, he was a French peasant whose father had fought as a mercenary and who encouraged him to do the same in America in hopes of scoring big payments and land in the new country. True or false? _____

45. As soon as the Declaration of Independence had been issued, the Congress set to work on the Articles of Confederation to unite the colonies. What was the hole in the document that made it difficult to run a country? _____

46. After several solid victories in 1777, General William Howe, the British commander-in-chief, instructed his men to treat civilians with kid gloves, and saw to it that his imported German soldiers did the same. True or false?_____

47. Name the British general who surrendered with his entire army after defeat in the Battle of Saratoga. (Five extra points for also naming the American general who scored the victory.)

_____

48. When he arrived from Germany to take over the training of the American military at Valley Forge, von Steuben, speaking little or no English, communicated his orders in:

   a. German
   b. French
   c. Pidgin
   d. Sign language

49. What country was first to go public with support of the American fight for independence from Great Britain?

   a. France
   b. Holland
   c. Spain
   d. Iceland

50. What was the Conway Cabal? _____

51. Who was the general who defied Washington's orders, traded insults with him, and ended up being arrested, court-martialed, and dismissed from his command for a year?

_____

52. Benedict Arnold's plot to turn over West Point to the British fell apart when his British contact was picked up carrying fatally incriminating plans written in Arnold's hand. Who was the contact, later hanged as a spy?

_____

54. I was a slave who allowed myself to be recruited as a British spy but was really a double agent. I relayed information about British troop movements and was instrumental in misleading the enemy with a false document, helping Washington and Lafayette to victory at Yorktown. Who am I?

_____

53. And where was he hiding the plans when he was caught?

_____

55. Name the British general who surrendered at the Siege of Yorktown, leading Parliament to shut down the war effort.

_____

56. In the aftermath of that battle, when the British general sent an aide to capitulate, he tried to avoid Washington and surrender instead to:

_____

57. Who, late in 1781, became the first President of Congress under the Articles of Confederation, which some insist makes him the rightful claimant to the title First President of the United States? (The job of leading the Congress changed hands on a yearly basis until the Constitution was written and ratified, in 1789.)

_____

58. I was a young woman in 1782, when some skirmishes were still taking place as the war came to a close. I disguised myself as a man to enlist in the army, and served for 17 months in the Light Infantry Company of the Fourth Massachusetts Regiment. I was wounded in battle near Tarrytown, New York, but managed to keep my secret. Who am I? _____

59. Who was the British Prime Minister who was pressured out of office by a no-confidence vote after he failed to persuade the colonies to accept a peace plan that didn't include independence?

_____

60. What were John Adams, Ben Franklin, and John Jay doing in a hotel room in Paris on September 3, 1783? _____

61. Who were they with? _____

62. Washington resigned his position as commander-in-chief on December 19, 1783. How did he hang it up?
   a. By letter to Congress
   b. By letter to more than two
      dozen possible successors
   c. By personal appearance
      before Congress meeting in Annapolis
   d. In a speech in front of the Liberty Bell

63. One reason Washington had been an attractive candidate for commander-in-chief is that he took the job without a salary, asking only for reimbursement of his expenses during the war. When he finally submitted an accounting, roughly how much did he request?

    a. $1,000
    b. $15,000
    c. $25,000
    d. $75,000

64. Who was Gilbert du Motier? _____

65. Americans whose allegiance to the King compelled them to flee to Canada or other British colonies at the end of the war were known as:

    a. United Empire Loyalists
    b. The British Faithful
    c. Kingdom of Great Britain Subjects in Exile
    d. Britons Abroad

66. Who is generally credited with devising the structure of the Constitution, and doing much of the drafting, including the first 10 amendments, the Bill of Rights?

    a. Thomas Jefferson
    b. James Madison
    c. Robert Morris
    d. Gouverneur Morris

67. Who was the wordsmith who also did much drafting and polishing, and is credited with the wording of the preamble?

_____

68. Who persuaded delegates to compromise on a bicameral legislative body, a House with members chosen according to population, to the benefit of larger states, and, for balance, a two-member-per-state Senate, giving weight to smaller states?

_____

69. By omitting references to God, the Constitution was following the pattern of the Articles of Confederation and, in fact, all of the state constitutions that preceded it. True or false?

_____

70. While the Constitution was being drafted, debated, and ratified, Thomas Jefferson was mostly out of the loop. Why?

_____

71. A series of articles written to urge ratification of the Constitution, known as the Federalist, appeared under what Latin byline?

_____

72. Who *isn't* credited with being a contributor to the Federalist?

    a. Alexander Hamilton
    b. John Jay
    c. James Madison
    d. William Patterson

73. Of the 13 colonies, three ratified the Constitution by unanimous vote. Ten points for any one you can name, and a bonus ten for each of the other two. _____

74. Who was the only representative to sign four key documents that led to the founding of the American nation: the Articles of Association (October 20, 1774), the Declaration of Independence (July 4, 1776), the Articles of Confederation (November 15, 1777), and the United States Constitution (September 17, 1787)?

75. George Washington won the presidency after a bitter campaign against such opponents as John Adams and Thomas Jefferson, but after several ballots Washington prevailed. True or false?

76. A Senate committee recommended one of the following as the proper form of address for the new leader:

   a. "President of the United States"
   b. "His Magnificence"
   c. "His Highness the President of the United States and Protector of their Liberties"
   d. "The Supremely Important Leader of the Entire Nation from Coast to Coast"

77. Who administered the oath of office to President Washington at the first inaugural? _____

78. Which artist produced the first known portrait of George Washington?

   a. Gilbert Stuart
   b. Charles Willson Peale
   c. John Singleton Copley
   d. Jean-Antoine Houdon

79. Which *wasn't* the name of a newspaper during the time of the Revolution?

  a. *Pennsylvania Packet*
  b. *Salem Gazette*
  c. *Charleston Picayune*
  d. *New York Journal*
  e. *The Independent Journal*

80. How did these battles go for the rebels, win or lose? Two points each.

  a. Battle of Harlem Heights: _____
  b. Battle of Bennington: _____
  c. Battle of Brandywine: _____
  d. Battle of Germantown: _____
  e. Battle of Stony Point: _____

81. How about these?

  a. Battle of Kettle Creek: _____
  b. Battle of Briar Creek: _____
  c. Siege of Savannah: _____
  d. Battle of Cowpens: _____
  e. Battle of Eutaw Springs: _____

82. What accomplished military man of the Revolution died in 1792 and was buried in Paris, until President Theodore Roosevelt had people track down his remains and bring them back to be honored with an elaborate black marble sarcophagus at the Naval Academy, Annapolis? _____

83. When was the Continental Army established?

    a. April 19, 1775
    b. June 14, 1775
    c. July 5, 1776
    d. September 16, 1776

84. As soon as the Continental Army was created, four men were named to the rank of major general, to serve next in line under the commander-in-chief: Artemas Ward, Charles Lee, Philip Schuyler, and Israel Putnam. Which of the four served throughout the war?

_____

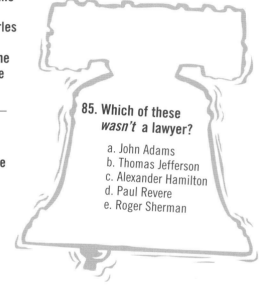

85. Which of these *wasn't* a lawyer?

    a. John Adams
    b. Thomas Jefferson
    c. Alexander Hamilton
    d. Paul Revere
    e. Roger Sherman

86. The first abolition association in America, the Society for the Relief of Free Negroes Unlawfully Held in Bondage, was formed April 14, 1775. Where?

    a. Princeton
    b. Cambridge
    c. New Haven
    d. Philadelphia

87. I signed the Declaration of Independence (although I wasn't really in favor at first), as well as the Articles of Confederation and the Constitution. But I'm better known for securing loans for the Continental Army. I may have profited a bit myself, but the soldiers got fed and got paid. That's why they call me "The Financier of the Revolution." Who am I? _____

88. **For two points each, who is credited with these well-known lines? Match.**

    a. "Give me liberty or give me death."   f. John Paul Jones
    b. "I regret that I have but one life   g. Benjamin Franklin
       to lose for my country."   h. Nathan Hale
    c. "These are the times that try   i. Patrick Henry
       men's souls."   j. Thomas Paine
    d. "I have not yet begun to fight."
    e. "We must all hang together, or
       assuredly we shall all hang separately."

89. **What did the names Bushrod and Burwell mean to George Washington?** _____

90. **Match the important persons on the left with their birthplaces on the right. Two points apiece.**

    a. George Washington   f. Massachusetts
    b. Alexander Hamilton   g. Maryland
    c. John Hancock   h. Nevis, West Indies
    d. Benedict Arnold   i. Virginia
    e. John Hanson   j. Connecticut

91. **For five points each, name the military leaders known by these nicknames:**

    a. "The Swamp Fox": _____
    b. "Light-Horse Harry": _____

92. **Speaking of "Light-Horse Harry," he was the eulogizer who wrote, on the death of George Washington in 1799, a line that's been quoted ever since. Finish it: "To the memory of the man . . ."**

    _____

93. What simple song, already well known at the time, was first used by British troops to mock the colonists but then turned on the British, quickly becoming an informal fight song for the Rebel soldiers and an anthem for America? _____

94. It all started in the Boston area, and the city of Boston was quickly taken by the royal military, in April 1775. How long was Boston occupied?

    a. 2 months
    b. 11 months
    c. 25 months
    d. 48 months

95. Who wrote the training manual known as "the blue book," officially titled *Regulations for the Order and Discipline of the Troops of the United States*? _____

96. When did Tadeusz Kościuszko arrive to join the effort as the Continental Army's chief engineer?

    a. late 1775
    b. shortly after July 4, 1776
    c. during the Valley Forge winter of 1777–78
    d. after the Siege of Charleston, in 1780

97. For five points each, what were the *Bonhomme Richard* and the *Vulture*? _____

98. I'm the illegitimate son of one of the Founding Fathers. Things were fine between us until all this talk about independence started. The King made me Royal Governor of New Jersey, so needless to say I was a steadfast Loyalist. I split with my father, and then his pals made me a POW for two years. As soon as I could, I went to England and never came back. My father cut me out of his will; so be it. Who am I? _____

99. Who first proposed the name "United States of America"?

   a. Thomas Jefferson
   b. Patrick Henry
   c. Richard Henry Lee
   d. Thomas Paine

100. A week after he had signed the Treaty of Paris, Benjamin Franklin wrote a friend back in the new United Sates of America: "The Definitive Treaty was signed the third instant. We are now friends with England, and with all Mankind! May we never see another War! for in my opinion, there never was a good war _____ _____ _____ _____."

ANSWERS

1. c.

2. The Stamp Act

3. Sons of Liberty (bonus: from Isaac Barré, a supportive British Parliament member who defended the rebellious actions of the colonists in a floor debate, calling them "these sons of Liberty")

4. b.

5. d.

6. a.

7. c. (to Castle Island)

8. Committees of Correspondence

9. The Dartmouth, the Eleanor, and the Beaver

10. c.

11. c.

12. a.

13. The Intolerable Acts

14. Philadelphia

15. b.

16. Peyton Randolph of Virginia (president of the Congress)

17. a.

18. William Dawes (bonus: Samuel Prescott)

19. He suspected his American-born wife, Margaret Kemble Gage, of leaking the Redcoats' plans to raid Lexington and Concord; to prevent a possible repeat he had her shipped to England

20. d. (Ralph Waldo Emerson, author of "Concord Hymn," who wrote that the "embattled farmers" had fired the shot)

21. b.

22. Breed's Hill

23. "Don't fire until you see the whites of their eyes."

24. a.

25. None; nor did any of the boys fire a weapon

26. c.

27. False—a proclamation of August 23, 1775, for example, declared "many of our subjects" to be "in open and avowed rebellion"

28. Continentals (as in the inflation-era expression "not worth a Continental")

29. *Common Sense*, by Thomas Paine

30. Abigail Adams, writing to John (who replied: "I cannot but laugh. . . . Depend upon it, we know better than to repeal our masculine systems . . . in practice, you know we are the subjects . . .")

31. d.

32. The Virginia Declaration of Rights (bonus: George Mason)

33. d. (from the Preamble to the United States Constitution)

34. a. John Adams, b. Thomas Jefferson, c. Benjamin Franklin, d. John Hancock, e. Samuel Adams

35. Stephen Hopkins

36. The Bible (Leviticus 25:10)

37. Silas Deane

38. d.

39. Destroyed boats up and down the river, forcing the British to wait for the river to freeze before pursuing them

40. b.

41. John Honeyman

42. a. and b.

43. 19

44. False—he was the real thing (although he renounced his title after the French Revolution)

45. No provision for taxing

46. False—widespread rough treatment was a key factor in reinvigorating a taste for independence in a population that had been tiring of the war

47. John Burgoyne (extra points: Horatio Gates)

48. b.

49. a.

50. A loose, and ultimately failing, effort among some Continental Army officers to have Washington deposed

51. Charles Lee

52. John André

53. In his boot

54. James Armistead

55. Charles Cornwallis

56. French General Rochambeau, who had arrived with 5,000 troops as part of France's assistance to the Revolutionary cause

57. John Hanson of Maryland

58. Deborah Sampson (later Deborah Sampson Gannett)

59. Lord North, who resigned half a year after the British defeat at Yorktown

60. Signing the Treaty of Paris, in which Britain recognized an independent United States and agreed to pull its troops out

61. David Hartley

62. c.

63. c.

64. The pro-American French general and diplomat known as Lafayette

65. a.

66. b.

67. Gouverneur Morris

68. Roger Sherman

69. False—the earlier documents did invoke a deity, so by choosing not to the writers of the Constitution broke new ground

70. He was in Paris, having replaced Franklin as minister to France

71. Publius

72. d.

73. Delaware (the first state to ratify), New Jersey, and Georgia

74. Roger Sherman of Connecticut

75. False—he was unopposed

76. c. (really; it was the House that suggested the simpler, less British-sounding a.)

77. Robert Livingston (as chancellor of the state of New York; the first capital was in New York City)

78. b.

79. c.

80. a. lose, b. win, c. lose, d. lose, e. win

81. a. win, b. lose, c. lose, d. win, e. lose

82. John Paul Jones

83. b.

84. None of them

85. d. (Revere was a silversmith)

86. d.

87. Robert Morris

88. a.-i., b.-h., c.-j., d.-f., e.-g.

89. Those were his nephews, Bushrod Washington, who became an associate justice of the U.S. Supreme Court (and who inherited Mount Vernon), and Burwell Bassett, who became a Congressman

90. a.-i., b.-h., c.-f., d.-j., e.-g.

91. a. Francis Marion, known for guerrilla tactics; b. Henry Lee III, cavalry officer and later governor of Virginia and a U.S. Congressman

92. "To the memory of the man, first in war, first in peace, and first in the hearts of his fellow-citizens" (usually rendered today as ". . . his countrymen")

93. "Yankee Doodle"

94. b.

95. The officer from Germany, Baron von Steuben

96. b.

97. When France gave a slow merchant vessel to Naval commander John Paul Jones, he overhauled it into a respectable warship and named it the *Bonhomme Richard* to honor Ben Franklin, whose *Poor Richard's Almanack* was known in France as *Les Maximes du Bonhomme Richard*; the *Vulture* was the British vessel that helped Benedict Arnold make his getaway after he was caught in the act

98. William Franklin

99. d.

100. "Or a bad peace"